CW00392483

FOLLOWING JESUS' LEADERSHIP

Learn How To
Lead Like Jesus

DR. STEPHEN SWIHART

All Scripture quotations are taken from
Holy Bible: New International Version. Copyright © 1973, 1978, 1984
International Bible Society. Used by permission of Zondervan Bible Publishers.

Master Plan Ministries
Dr. Stephen Swihart   1333 El Reno Street   Elkhart, IN 46516
(574) 294-1995   www.masterplanministries.com

Contents

How to Use This Book

Encountering God . . . for Real

Throughout this volume I want you to think outside the traditional box for a Bible study. For example, I don't want you to *read* through this book. And I don't want you to *study* it either. There is something more profound than *reading* and *studying*. Your higher goal must always be *encountering!*

The success of this book, and for that matter the success of the Bible, depends on you literally *encountering God* as the greater result of your reading and studying. In other words there is more to Bible devotions than learning spiritual truths; there is *encountering* the God we read about and study.

Tuck this important truth down deep inside your heart: ***One experience with God is better than a thousand explanations about Him!*** Repeat this simple line three or four more times. Let it sink in. Then ponder this possibility: as you go through this material you can do more than learn facts; you can literally *experience* what it means to walk closely with the Lord, and you can also *experience* what it means to lead others into this same intimacy with the Lord!

Honestly, one of the largest problems among many Christian leaders is the fact that while they *believe* sincerely in God, they infrequently *encounter* Him or lead others into *experiences* with Him. This is a problem that needs to be fixed.

In this book you are going to discover that leadership from Jesus' perspective primarily means living a life of intimacy with God: experiencing His presence, performing His will, and explaining to others how they can enter into a life-changing relationship with God. The goal of leadership is not *education,* but *transformation.* It isn't enough to *learn* about God; we must also become people who know how to *lean* on God for everything!

The Christian life is not so much about trying to be a good person as it is about learning how to walk with God, with Jesus, and with the Holy Spirit moment by moment. Then, when we discover how to *follow God well,* we will find the secrets of how to *lead others well.*

Leadership is not about getting people to attend your church or to participate in countless Bible studies. Leadership is about *transformation* — your transformation, and the transformation of the people you lead. Leadership is about helping people experience the Lord by knowing the *desires* of His heart, the *thoughts* of His mind, the *words* from His mouth, and the *decisions* of His will.

Therefore, when you go through this book, don't settle for merely filling in the blanks. And if you are leading someone else through this material, don't be content with simply getting them to jot down their ideas here and there on each page. Aim higher. Personally expect to meet with God in every lesson, and equally expect your co-learners to connect with God personally as well!

Consult Bible Commentaries and Bible Dictionaries

If it is possible, you should examine a commentary or Bible dictionary several times in each lesson in order to gain additional insights. If you do not have these tools, borrow them or check them out of your local library. Put these titles on your shopping list, and purchase them when you are able. The following reference books are worth owning and using frequently:

- *The Bible Knowledge Commentary (Old and New Testaments)* - two volumes, edited by John Walvoord and Roy Zuck (Victor Books).

- *The Bible Exposition Commentary* - two volumes on the New Testament, by Warren W. Wiersbe (Victor Books).

- *Nelson's New Illustrated Bible Dictionary,* edited by R. Youngblood, F. F. Bruce and R. K. Harrison (Nelson).

- *The New International Dictionary of the Bible,* edited by J. D. Douglas and Merrill C. Tenney (Zondervan Publishing House).

Ask your pastor for additional suggestions.

Maintain a Fourfold Strategy

Sometimes the secret to success in devotions is as simple as following a basic structure. Here are four guidelines we have found to be essential for meaningful and consistent devotions:

- Meet with the Lord at a specific *period* every day. Ask the Lord when He would like you to meet with Him.

- Meet with Him at a specific *place* that is suitable for both study and meditation.

- Follow a specific *plan* for your times with the Lord. For example, you might focus on study in the mornings and pray in the evenings (or something else).

- Find a specific *partner* (or group) with whom you will share your discoveries and questions — be accountable to someone.

Take your time with these lessons. This is not a race. The goal is not to go through this book, but to let this book become an instrument in helping you experience God's presence, conviction, comfort and transformation. Do your best to make your responses as *thorough* and *personal* as possible. Have holy and happy devotions!

1. Profound Humility

 Whoever wants to become great among you must be your servant, and whoever wants to be first must be your slave — just as the Son of Man did not come to be served, but to serve, and to give his life as a ransom for many — Matthew 20:26b-28.

Before you can *lead* others successfully, you must first learn how to *follow* successfully. And before you can follow well, you must learn how to be humble. Never forget this all-important fact: **Humility is the primary root beneath every spiritual accomplishment!** Repeat this statement to yourself over and over, day after day. All of your success in the Lord depends on this chief character quality!

Jesus was the most humble person ever to live on earth. From start to finish, he knew that a humble disposition was the key to bringing glory to God and goodness to people. Therefore, it is reasonable that he requires a profound level of humility from everyone he calls to serve him.

The Example of Jesus - Part 1

Jesus is your perfect role model for the kind of humility that God expects and rewards. Open your Bible and carefully study Jesus' example in Philippians 2:5-11. Pick apart each phrase of this passage (consult commentaries for extra insights). In the space below itemize how Jesus practiced profound humility. Also, ask God for fresh insights and applications. Write out what He tells you.

The Example of Jesus - Part 2

I used to think that God's gifts were on shelves one above the other and that the taller we grew in Christian character the more easily we could reach them. I now find that God's gifts are on shelves one beneath the other and that it is not a question of growing taller but of stooping lower — F. B. Meyer.

Look to Jesus again. He knew how to get God's attention and how to gain His favor; we must learn the same thing. If you and I are going to be anything like Jesus, and if we are going to experience effective leadership, then we will need to learn deeper levels of humility. How does Jesus demonstrate the purest kind of humility in the following passages? What do you find here that should take you to your knees every day? What do you find here that you should impart to others?

Matthew 20:20-28	Luke 22:39-44

The Confrontation of Jesus

For those who would learn God's ways, humility is the first thing, humility is the second, and humility is the third — Augustine.

Before Jesus calls ordinary humans like you and me to serve in the Kingdom of God, he knows something we need to know better than anything else: **God only extends His supernatural grace for effective leadership to humble souls!** This fact is crucial because it informs us that Jesus will be quick to tap us on the shoulder (or thump us on our chest, or worse!) if we become misdirected into thinking we can serve God effectively with our own abilities or our own agendas. For example, what did Jesus say in Matthew 23:1-12 that should scare every leader half to death? Be specific and practical in how you can apply this passage both to yourself and to those you lead.

The Root Beneath Spiritual Success

You can be certain that from God's perspective no one's success is large in whose heart He finds pride, and no one's achievement is small in whose heart He finds humility. People in the world and even people in the church often judge greatness by what they can see on the *outside,* but the Lord always measures it by what He can see on the *inside.* We might fool others with our seeming success, and we might even fool ourselves, but we will never fool God. Now, slowly read through Hebrews 12:1-3 three or four times. Examine it closely. Consult a commentary or two. Then, write out at least three key leadership principles the Lord wants you to make based on these words.

Putting It Together

Humility can be *taught accurately,* but it is rarely reproduced until it is *demonstrated consistently.* Therefore, a leader's best teaching tool is his (or her) personal example. How you reverence the Godhead in private and in public, and how you truly humble yourself to help people will determine whether or not you will gain their favor. Without this favor you may have a leadership title, but you will not operate with a genuine leader's influence. Don't trick yourself into believing that you deserve respect; this must be earned via the many proofs of personal humility. In the space below, write out a thoughtful prayer for the growth of the grace of humility.

2. Steadfast Priorities

Seek first his kingdom and his righteousness, and all these things will be given to you as well — Matthew 6:33.

Jesus knew what mattered most to God, and he managed to maintain his focus on those precise things every moment of the day and night. He never majored on minors or minored on majors.

Jesus Lived to Fulfill God's Priorities

The *last* thing most people learn in life is what they should have been putting *first* all along. Jesus didn't have that difficulty. He knew what was truly important. Look closely at Deuteronomy 6:4-9, Leviticus 19:9-18 and Mark 12:28-34. Also, read your commentary on these passages. Then, based on these texts, explain what it means to love God and people as your top priorities.

On an ascending scale of 1 to 10, how concerned is the world around you about fulfilling God's two chief priorities?

A.	In television programs?	_____	H.	In grocery stores?	_____
B.	In the newspaper?	_____	I.	In restaurants?	_____
C.	In government legislation?	_____	J.	In gas stations?	_____
D.	In public schools?	_____	K.	In video stores?	_____
E.	In the average business?	_____	L.	In your doctor's office?	_____
F.	In the police department?	_____	M.	In your job?	_____
G.	In shopping malls?	_____	N.	In your neighborhood?	_____

Based on your responses, how serious is *your world* about honoring God's priorities?

_____

Jesus Loved God Supremely

The highest priority that consistently motivated Jesus was his passion to please his heavenly Father all of the time and in every conceivable way. Ponder the weightiness of this inner drive in Jesus. This means that in all of his *desires, thoughts, speech, and decisions* Jesus put God's interests before his own interests! That's love — profound love! In the verses below Jesus explains the precise nature of his love for God. Read these passages and identify what loving God meant to Jesus.

John 5:30	John 8:29	John 14:31

Is this the way *you* love God? Is this the way you are teaching others to love God? Where does your personal love and your teaching of love need to be deepened? Be specific.

Jesus Loved People Passionately

It's accurate to say that Jesus loves *the world,* but he didn't come to earth to hug a tree and save the *planet.* Instead, he came to die on a tree and to save *people!* Jesus is in the *people* business. This means that when Jesus came to earth he had *you* in his mind. How do the following passages demonstrate Jesus' love for people, *and for you in particular?*

Matthew 20:25-28 with Romans 5:6-8 _____

_____

_____

_____

_____

_____

_____

John 14:1-3 _____

_____

_____

_____

_____

_____

John 14:15-21 with 15:9-15 _____

_____

_____

_____

_____

_____

_____

Putting It Together

Earlier you evaluated *the world* on how seriously it takes its priority to love God and people. Now, you will evaluate yourself, because your ability to lead others into a deeper love for God and people is directly proportional to your personal hunger for a greater life of love:

A. Do you end each day by spending time with the Lord? Explain.

B. Do you begin each day by spending time with the Lord? Explain.

C. To what degree have you surrendered to the Lord the *desires* of your heart, the *thoughts* of your mind, the *words* of your mouth, and the *decisions* of your will? Explain.

D. How aware are you of the (1) spiritual, (2) physical, and (3) emotional wellbeing of your family? How involved are you in their total wellbeing? How would *they* answer these questions about you? Explain.

E. How aware are you of the (1) spiritual, (2) physical, and (3) emotional wellbeing of the people at your place of work (or school)? How involved are you in their total wellbeing? How would *they* answer these questions about you? Explain.

3. Significant Prayer Habits

 Very early in the morning, while it was still dark, Jesus got up, left the house and went off to a solitary place, where he prayed — Mark 1:35.

In ORDINARY prayer we rely on God's *ears* to hear us when we speak to Him. In EXTRAORDINARY prayer we also rely on God's *mouth* to speak to us as we listen to Him. When these two types of prayer are combined, we have SIGNIFICANT prayer. And this is precisely the kind of praying that Jesus experienced. More than that, it is also the kind of prayer that God wants you to experience, especially as a leader!

The Prayer Life of Jesus - Part 1

Look up the following passages dealing with Jesus' own prayer life, and fill in the blanks. Then, to the right side of the passage, pray and write out what you hear the Lord telling you about applying these verses. (These quotations are taken from the New International Version of the Bible.)

Mark 1:35

Very _____ in the morning,
while it was still _____,
Jesus _____ _____, left the house
and went off to a _____ place,
where he prayed.

Luke 5:16

Jesus _____ withdrew
to _____ places
and prayed.

Hebrews 5:7

During the days of Jesus' life on earth,
he offered up prayers and petitions
with _____ _____ and
_____ to the one who could save
him from death, and he was _____
because of his _____ _____ .

What the Lord is Saying to Me:

15

The Prayer Life of Jesus - Part 2

Luke 3:21-22

When all the people were being baptized, Jesus was _____ too. And as he was _____ , heaven was opened and the Holy Spirit descended on him . . . And a _____ came from heaven: "You are My Son . . ."

Luke 6:12

One of those days Jesus went out to a _____ side to pray, and spent the _____ praying to God.

Matthew 26:39-44

Going a little farther, he _____ with his face to the _____ and prayed, "My Father, if it is possible, may this cup be taken from me. Yet not as ___ _____ , but as _____ _____ ."

Mark 11:15-17

On reaching Jerusalem, Jesus entered the temple area and began _____ _____ those who were _____ and _____ there. He _____ the tables of the money changers and the benches of those selling doves, and would not allow anyone to carry _____ through the temple. And as he taught them, he said, "Is it not written: 'My house will be called a house of _____ for all nations'?"

Luke 22:31-32a

"Simon, Simon, Satan has _____ to sift you as wheat. But I have _____ for you, Simon, that your _____ may not fail.

What the Lord is Saying to Me:

Jesus Enjoyed Intimacy with God

Jesus relied on the Father's *ears* to hear him when he prayed (as you saw in the previous two pages). But he also relied on the Father's *mouth* to speak to him as he waited in prayer (as you will see on this and the next page). It was this side of prayer, hearing the voice of God, that enabled Jesus to become an effective leader.

Jesus did not pray to God or minister to others on his own initiative or out of his own ideas. Instead, he waited on God for his prayers and for his ministry assignments. Jesus never got ahead of God. Instead, he listened and he followed the directions that God spoke to him. As you read the following verses, write out a heart-felt prayer that is based on each passage.

John 5:19

John 6:38

John 7:16

17

Putting It Together

Regardless of how many times you have prayed, even if it has been for decades, there are still new depths, insights and experiences to receive. Therefore, you and I must always press forward for more. What do you see in the following passages about Jesus' prayers that are especially important for a leader? Explain with examples.

John 12:49-50

John 14:10

John 14:24b

The Wrap Up

No one perfectly listens to or hears from God. No one. Therefore, we must always be ready to lay our ideas before the Word of God and other mature Christian leaders. A good leader will be glad to have his thoughts tested because he is acutely aware of the danger of self-deception!

4. Constant Reliance on the Holy Spirit

The one whom God has sent speaks the words of God, for
God gives the Spirit [to him] without limit — John 3:34.

The Holy Spirit in Jesus' Life - Part 1

The secret to Jesus' success was not due to the fact that he was Divine — he gave up all of his Divine prerogatives when he chose to take on our humanity (Philippians 2:5-11)! Instead, Jesus' powerful messages and miracles were the direct result of the Holy Spirit working in his life! Understanding this fact is crucial. Look up the following references and write out how Jesus' life was empowered by the Holy Spirit from beginning to end. How should this information impact you as a leader?

Matthew 1:18-20 with Luke 1:35	Matthew 4:1 with John 5:30
Luke 3:21-22 with John 1:32-34 and 3:34	Hebrews 5:15 with 9:14

The Holy Spirit in Jesus' Life - Part 2

Every aspect of Jesus' ministry is indebted to the anointing of the Holy Spirit working in and through him. Think about it: as an ordinary man his abilities were extremely limited, but with the empowerment from the Holy Spirit Jesus could significantly impact lives! What lessons about effective leadership can you discover in the following passages?

His Teaching Ministry: See Luke 4:18 with Acts 1:1-2 and Acts 20:25-32.

_____

_____

_____

_____

His Healing Ministry: See Luke 5:17 with James 5:14-16.

_____

_____

_____

_____

His Exorcism Ministry: See Matthew 12:26 with Mark 16:17a.

_____

_____

_____

_____

His Total Ministry: See Acts 10:34-38 with Matthew 28:18-20.

_____

_____

_____

_____

The Gifts of the Holy Spirit in Jesus' Life

As a human being, Jesus could perform no miracles. He could not heal the sick, cast demons from people, walk on water, know people's thoughts, or many other things. But with special gifts from the Spirit, Jesus was able to perform numerous miracles. Look up six or seven passages from the following list and notice how specific gifts from the Spirit operated in Jesus' life.

THE GIFTS	IN JESUS' LIFE	THE GIFTS	IN JESUS' LIFE
Apostle Ephesians 4:11	Hebrews 3:1	**Faith** 1 Corinthians 12:7-11	Matthew 21:18-22
Prophet Ephesians 4:11	Deuteronomy 18:15 Mark 6:1-6	**Gifts of healing** 1 Corinthians 12:7-11	Matthew 4:23-24
Evangelist Ephesians 4:11	Matthew 4:18-20 Luke 19:10	**Miraculous powers** 1 Corinthians 12:7-11	Mark 6:45-52
Pastor / Shepherd Ephesians 4:11	1 Peter 5:1-4	**Prophecy** 1 Corinthians 12:7-11	Matthew 24:1-8
Teacher Ephesians 4:11	Acts 1:1-2	**Distinguishing spirits** 1 Corinthians 12:7-11	Mark 9:14-29
Leader Romans 12:6-8	Matthew 10:1-16	**Serving/Helping** Romans 12:6-8	Matthew 20:28
Administration 1 Corinthians 12:28	Mark 6:35-44	**Encouraging** Romans 12:6-8	Matthew 10:17-20
Word of wisdom 1 Corinthians 12:7-11	Matthew 21:23-27	**Giving** Romans 12:6-8	Matthew 15:29-39
Word of knowledge 1 Corinthians 12:7-11	Mark 2:8	**Mercy** Romans 12:6-8	Matthew 9:35-38

As a leader, do you know your gift and how to use it in a supernatural way?

_____

_____

_____

Putting It Together

In order to become a *Christian*, you must first have a proper relationship with *Christ*. And in order to become *spiritual,* you must first have a proper relationship with the *Spirit*. Your success in serving the Lord depends entirely on these two relationships. In the space below, describe your current relationship with both the Lord Jesus Christ and the Holy Spirit.

    A. Your relationship with the Lord Jesus Christ:

    B. Your relationship with the Holy Spirit:

5. Aggressive Spiritual Warfare

 He who does what is sinful is of the devil, because the devil has been sinning from the beginning. The reason the Son of God appeared was to destroy the devil's work — 1 John 3:8.

In the western world there is great reluctance to take demons and invisible powers seriously, even though witches, wizards and magic are immensely popular in movies, television and books. In the Bible, however, the devil and evil forces are taken literally and with great seriousness. In fact, the subjects of Satan (or the devil) and demons are mentioned more than 100 times in the four Gospels alone!

Jesus took demons and their work so seriously that he confronted them almost everywhere he traveled. He could detect them when they corrupted people's minds and when they afflicted their bodies. He could also order them to cease their activities. And more than that, Jesus expected his followers (especially his leaders) to overcome Satan's works as well.

The Devil Attacks Jesus

Jesus could not defeat the devil when he attacked others until he first defeated the devil in his own life. Based on Matthew 4:1-11, how did Satan attack Jesus, and how did Jesus defeat him? Make a personal application for each temptation.

A. The First Temptation 4:1-4

B. The Second Temptation 4:5-7

C. The Third Temptation 4:8-11

Jesus Attacks the Devil - Part 1

Jesus confronted and conquered the devil's works nearly everywhere he went (Acts 10:38; 1 Jn. 3:8). Clearly, his *experience* is our *example.* Look up the following references and identify (1) who is demonized, (2) the characteristics of the demonic activity, and (3) the manner in which Jesus deals with Satan and Satan's victims. Make at least one practical observation you can apply from each of the episodes on this and the following page.

Luke 13:10-16   Matthew 12:22-28   Mark 9:14-29

Jesus Attacks the Devil - Part 2

Matthew 8:28-34	Luke 11:14-26
Mark 1:21-28	Acts 10:34-38

Putting It Together

Jesus' ministry was a "show-n-tell" experience for the disciples. They watched. They listened. And then they were ordered to reproduce what they had seen and heard. Read the following passages, and carefully record how the early believers dealt with demons. In each example write out one practical principle for yourself and your work as a leader.

Luke 9:1-6, 10

_____

_____

_____

Luke 10:1-4, 17-20

_____

_____

_____

Mark 16:15-20

_____

_____

_____

Acts 4:23-31 with Acts 5:12, 16; 8:4-10; 13:1-12 and 16:16-18.

_____

_____

_____

_____

_____

_____

_____

_____

6. A Heart for People

When he [Jesus] saw the crowds, he had compassion on them, because they were harassed and helpless, like sheep without a shepherd — Matthew 9:36.

Jesus loved people. It's that simple and that profound. Everywhere he went, he had time for people — to *teach* them and to *touch* them.

If your own leadership is going to reach its maximum fruitfulness, it will be because you practiced the grace of giving yourself wholly away for the benefit of others (beginning at home, moving to the church, and then extending to the whole world).

How Jesus Demonstrated His Love - Part 1

Jesus was so devoted to helping people that at times he even neglected eating so he could serve more people (Mk. 3:20). In the space below (and on the next page as well), identify some of the specific ways Jesus proved that his love for people was real. In each of these examples ask the Lord for one critical key you can apply.

Matthew 9:35-36	Mark 1:40-42

How Jesus Demonstrated His Love - Part 2

Here are more examples from Jesus and more opportunities for you to show people the full measure of your own love. How would the Lord like you to apply each of these episodes? And how would He like you to train others in the art of compassion?

Luke 4:38-41	Matthew 11:28-30
Luke 7:11-17	John 10:10-18

Who Received Jesus' Love

It is one thing to love the people who first love you, but it is another matter altogether to love people who have not yet loved you and may never love you. Jesus always took the initiative to love others. And he extended his compassion to every kind of person in every imaginable situation. As you examine the following references, notice the *types* of people Jesus helped:

A. Matthew 4:23 _____

B. Matthew 14:34-36 _____

C. Matthew 15:29-31 _____

D. Mark 2:13-17 _____

E. Mark 6:31-44 _____

F. Mark 7:31-35 _____

G. Mark 8:22-26 _____

H. Luke 7:36-50 _____

I. Luke 8:1-3 _____

J. Luke 8:40-42, 49-55 _____

Love is not measured by motives or sincerity, but by involvement.
Take a moment to reflect on your own level of love for people.
How deeply are you involved in peoples' lives?

Putting It Together

Jesus loved people on more than an emotional level. He also loved them on a spiritual level. That is, he loved them with the specific intention of helping them become pure and strong in the Lord. His love would confront sin in a person's life and provide a correction for it. In fact, at the end of Jesus' life when he washed the disciples' feet, he was doing a great deal more than demonstrating humility. He was primarily showing them the spiritual responsibility they had to keep one another free from daily sins. Read John 13:1-17, then answer the following questions.

First, what was the attitude in the disciples that prompted Jesus' action? See Luke 22:24-30.

Second, what did Jesus mean when he said that the disciples were "bathed" but still needed their feet to be "washed"? See John 13:6-11.

Third, notice that Jesus instructs each of his disciples to wash one another's feet. If dirty feet represent pride (or any other sin), how is one believer to "wash" the feet of another believer? See John 13:12-16.

Fourth, what is the promise Jesus gives to the person who will follow his counsel? See John 13:17.

Fifth, how does the Lord want you to lead others in the "washing" of feet?

7. A Soulwinning Passion

 The Son of Man came to seek and to save what was lost
— Luke 19:10.

Jesus was a bold soulwinner, and he trained his disciples to be equally aggressive. Why? Because he understood the one overwhelming fact that many people in the world and in the church so quickly forget: *Hell requires no reservation; heaven does!*

The greatest good that one person can do for another human being is to persuade him of his need for salvation and to convince him that the Savior, Jesus Christ, can permanently remove all of his sins! There are many other needs we may meet, but none compare in importance to this one.

Jesus was a Soulwinner

Soulwinning occupies such a large part of Jesus' life that this mission is even present in his name (Matthew 1:20-21). The name "Jesus" means "Yahweh [or the LORD] is our salvation." From start to finish, the Bible identifies Jesus' main task as one of rescuing souls. How is this leadership goal demonstrated in the following references?

John 3:1-15	Luke 19:1-10

The Gospel of John and the Mission of Jesus

In John's writing, more than any other Gospel, Jesus' mission of bringing salvation to sinners is repeatedly revealed. Closely examine these passages, keeping one idea at the front of your mind: *How can you become a more effective soulwinner?* Ask God to help you find at least one practical insight you can apply from each of the following passages.

1:10-13 _____
_____
_____
_____

1:29 _____
_____
_____
_____

3:16-18 _____
_____
_____
_____

4:1-26 _____
_____
_____
_____

5:24-27 _____
_____
_____
_____

6:32-40 _____
_____
_____
_____

12:23-28 _____
_____
_____
_____

14:6 (with Acts 4:12) _____
_____
_____
_____

17:1-3 _____
_____
_____
_____

20:30-31 _____
_____
_____
_____

He who wins souls is wise - Proverbs 11:30

Putting It Together

Winning a single person to Christ is one thing; winning the whole world is another matter altogether. When Jesus came to earth, he did not come to save a few souls here and there. He came to win *everyone*. In order for this to happen, he knew that he would need to train people to become soulwinners, and these soulwinners would need to train more people to be soulwinners, and so on. In the light of this mission, answer the following leadership questions.

A. When Jesus called his first disciples to follow him, what did he say he would train them to become? What are *you* training people to become? See Mark 1:16-17.

B. When Jesus saw the large crowds of people who needed to be saved, what instructions did he give to his disciples? What instructions are *you* giving to your followers? See Matthew 9:37-38.

C. When Jesus finished his ministry on earth, what commission did he give to his followers? How seriously do *your* followers take this commission? See Matthew 28:19-20?

Bishop John Tanner used to test chaplains with this question: ***If I had two minutes to live, how would you tell me to get to heaven?*** If they couldn't tell him in two minutes, he knew they couldn't tell him in two hours. How would *you* answer this question? Write out your reply in the space below.

**Do you know how to lead a person to Christ using "The Roman Road?"
See Romans 3:23; 6:23; 5:8 and 10:9-10, 13.**

8. Commitment to High Standards

 He [Jesus] said to them all: "If anyone would come after me, he must deny himself and take up his cross daily and follow me — Luke 9:23.

Jesus lived by the highest possible standards. He consistently gave his best, and he demanded that those who would follow him give their best as well. There was never any place for lukewarmness in Jesus' life or in the lives of those who sought to be his disciples.

Jesus Lived Totally for the Glory of God

The Lord Jesus Christ did not place any demand on others that he himself did not practice. He did more than "talk the talk." He also "walked the walk." Look up the following passages, and explain the nature of Jesus' commitment to excellence. Write out a leadership application for each point.

John 4:34 _____

_____

_____

John 5:30 _____

_____

_____

John 8:29 _____

_____

_____

Luke 22:42 _____

_____

_____

Hebrews 4:14-16 _____

_____

_____

Jesus Called His Disciples to Live Totally for the Glory of God - Part 1

Look at the passages below, and clarify *in personal terms* what the Lord is looking for in the people who want to follow him. Explain how your life demonstrates each of these passages.

Luke 9:23

Luke 14:25-35	Matthew 10:34-39	Matthew 7:21-27

Jesus Called His Disciples to Live Totally for the Glory of God - Part 2

The early church was far from perfect. In fact, in the book of Revelation Jesus confronts the Christians in five out of seven churches for falling short of his standards. Dig into these accounts and identify the problems that grieved the Lord. Explain how these same flaws appear today as well.

Revelation 2:1-7 _____

_____

_____

_____

_____

Revelation 2:12-17 _____

_____

_____

_____

_____

Revelation 2:18-29 _____

_____

_____

_____

_____

Revelation 3:1-6 _____

_____

_____

_____

_____

Revelation 3:14-22 _____

_____

_____

_____

_____

Putting It Together

I go out to preach with two propositions in mind.
First, every person ought to give his life to Christ.
Second, whether or not anyone else will give him his life, I will give him mine
— Jonathan Edwards.

In order to enlarge your impact on people, you may need to enlarge your commitment to people. What does the Lord want you to do in the following areas? Don't just jot down the first thing that comes to your mind; pray until you believe you have God's own response.

A. Regularly praying for specific sinners.

B. Regularly visiting specific sinners.

C. Regularly praying for specific Christians.

D. Regularly visiting specific Christians.

E. Regularly training key people and releasing them for ministry.

9. *Passionate and Skillful Teaching*

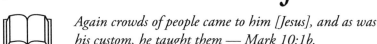

Again crowds of people came to him [Jesus], and as was his custom, he taught them — Mark 10:1b.

More than anything else, the devil is a teacher of lies (Gen. 3:1-5; Jn. 8:44). And more than anything else, Jesus is a teacher of the truth. In synagogue after synagogue, on mountain plateaus, from a seat in a boat, in the temple day after day, along the road, in living rooms — everywhere Jesus went — he was a passionate and skillful teacher. *Teaching was his number one business!*

The Sermon on the Mount - Part 1

The longest single teaching we have from Jesus is found in Matthew 5, 6 and 7 — the Sermon on the Mount. Read chapter 5, along with a commentary, and identify the main points in his message. How can you *train* others to live these verses? Be practical and specific.

_____

_____

_____

_____

_____

_____

_____

_____

_____

_____

_____

_____

_____

_____

_____

_____

_____

The Sermon on the Mount — Part 2

When Jesus looked at people, he could not only see them, he could see through them. Jesus knew what was in the heart of his audience members, and he often spoke to people about issues they would not be willing to bring up in public, like hypocrisy and financial needs. In this way his teachings were intensely relevant. Read Matthew 6 and record three major truths that are good for all time. How does the Lord want you not merely to teach, but to *train* others in these messages?

1

2

3

The Sermon on the Mount — Part 3

No other work of Jesus compares in frequency or importance to his ministry of teaching. And no other work created more trouble for him. When Jesus spoke, some people praised God, but others got angry and plotted to kill him! Study Matthew 7 and explain how these teachings would *inform* some and *inflame* others. Also, explain how today's Christian leaders must teach with a fear of God in their hearts and not a fear of man (even if a threat of unemployment or a hate crime law is thrown in their face).

Putting It Together

Generally speaking, there is far too little in-depth teaching in the typical church. Many Sunday morning messages are fireside chats without much of a fire! Sunday night and midweek messages are virtually absent altogether. Contrast this pattern with how the early church and the apostle Paul envisioned the importance of teaching. What leadership principles do you find here you can apply right away?

Acts 2:29-47	Acts 20:17-38

10. Devotion to a Team

Jesus went up on a mountainside and called to him those he wanted, and they came to him — Mark 3:13.

It has been said that the single most important word in our language is this: "We." The least important word is "I." It is significant to discover that Jesus was a "we" oriented person. He did not think in singular terms, but in the plural. Although he was the Leader of all leaders, he viewed himself as the first link in a circle of human links. He surrounded himself with people, trained them, and trusted them to carry on his work after he was gone. Much of Jesus' success is due to the fact that he prepared successors.

Developing a Team

After spending a whole night in prayer, Jesus hand-picked his own team! They didn't volunteer, and he didn't review resumes looking for the "sharpest tack." Instead, he prayed, and he heard from the Father whom he was to select to work at his side. Read this episode in Luke 6:12-16 and Mark 3:13-19 (be sure to notice the two key words, "with him," in Mark 3:14). In the space below explain how you can duplicate this pattern today. Why would this be a smart decision for you to make?

Jesus did much more than conduct Bible studies and business meetings for his hand-picked disciples. He was committed to *training* them and *equipping* them for successful spiritual ministry. How is this fact brought out in Matthew 4:18-22 and Ephesians 4:11-16? What implications do you see in this practice for your own training of others?

Making Your Team Successful

Jesus did not surround himself with a team so they would make *him* fruitful. Instead, he circled himself with a team so he could make *them* fruitful. How is this explained by Jesus in John 15:1-16? Think of at least two practical ways this information will impact your own leadership?

_____

_____

_____

_____

_____

_____

_____

_____

_____

_____

_____

_____

_____

_____

_____

_____

_____

_____

_____

_____

_____

_____

_____

_____

_____

_____

_____

_____

_____

_____

_____

Refining the Character of Your Team

There is more to leadership than sharing coffee and donuts among friends. Occasionally, Jesus found it necessary to confront his disciples, both individually and collectively. What did Jesus see in his team members that caused him to point out their mistakes? Do you have the boldness that is required to confront and correct people? How can you apply this lesson?

Matthew 14:25-31	Matthew 16:21-23	Mark 9:14-29

Luke 8:22-25	Luke 9:51-56

At times Jesus' disciples behaved shamefully, but Jesus would not give up on them if their hearts were prepared to repent and follow. How is this key leadership principle seen in Jesus' relationship with Peter? See Luke 22:31-34, 54-62 and John 21:15-19. How can you apply this point?

Putting It Together

After Jesus sent out the twelve disciples, they reported back to him on their work (Mk. 6:7-13, 30). And after Jesus sent out the seventy-two, they also reported back to him how their ministry went (Lk. 10:1-20). How should you incorporate this principle of follow up and accountability with your own team of disciples?

_____

_____

_____

_____

_____

_____

Jesus accepted, and even defended, the ministry of others outside of the circle of the twelve disciples. How is this practice relevant today within your own community and denomination? How can a narrow-minded devotion to only our own group prevent you from respecting and utilizing the larger body of Christ? See Mark 9:38-41.

_____

_____

_____

_____

_____

_____

In Jesus' team there were more than twelve men. Who else served Jesus, and how did they help? See Matthew 27:55-56 and Luke 8:1-3. Develop an important leadership principle you can apply from these texts.

_____

_____

_____

_____

_____

_____

11. No Fear of People

*I [Jesus] have come to bring fire on the earth, and how
I wish it were already kindled — Luke 12:49.*

On almost every page of the Gospels, Jesus is confronted by someone — usually a spiritually dead religious leader who is addicted to his man-made traditions, rather than to God's eternal truth. These leaders had big titles and even larger appetites to keep Jesus from rocking the boat and upsetting their lifeless way of doing things. But Jesus was never swayed by people in positions of power or by personal ambition. His interest was the truth, and if that offended people, he would not retreat. Jesus had no fear of people, because he had a overriding fear of God! Today's leaders will need a large dose of the same wholesome fear!

In this lesson you are going to do only one thing: *Discover how Jesus confronted and corrected people.* This is perhaps the least attractive aspect of leadership, but it is one of the most critical. If error in either *beliefs* or *behavior* is ignored, then corruption will rapidly multiply. Therefore, leaders must learn how to deal with misbeliefs and misbehavior. Look up the passages in this lesson, and identify at least one firm leadership principle in each section.

John 2:13-17 (at the beginning of his ministry)	Mark 11:15-18 (at the end of his ministry)	Mark 7:1-13 (throughout his ministry)

Confrontation Continued

Matthew 11:20-24 _____
_____
_____
_____
_____
_____
_____

Matthew 16:5-12 _____
_____
_____
_____
_____
_____
_____

Matthew 18:15-18 _____
_____
_____
_____
_____
_____
_____

Matthew 21:33-46 _____
_____
_____
_____
_____
_____
_____

Luke 11:37-54

Luke 12:49-56

Luke 13:10-17

John 6:25-66, 70-71

Putting It Together

The early church followed Jesus' example in confronting, rebuking and even removing members from their congregations. Look up these passages and explain why this sort of work must be part of every leader's occupation.

1 Corinthians 5:1-13

_____

_____

_____

_____

Romans 16:17-18

_____

_____

_____

_____

Titus 3:10-11

_____

_____

_____

_____

2 Thessalonians 3:6-15

_____

_____

_____

_____

Can you think of anyone who is causing problems among your friends or in your church? Should they be confronted and corrected? If so, what are you going to do?

12. Determination to Finish the Mission

 As the time approached for him [Jesus] to be taken up to heaven, Jesus resolutely set out for Jerusalem — Luke 9:51.

Winston Churchill once delivered a commencement address that no one has ever forgotten. This is all he said: "Never, never, never, never give up!" Everyone in the audience rose to their feet and gave a rousing applause. Jesus had that same conquering spirit within him. He was not a quitter. He knew Who sent him, he understood the mission, and he was determined to finish the job.

Surprises in the Ministry

Jesus knew there would be tough days in the ministry — it comes with the territory. But knowing in advance that there will be difficulties doesn't automatically remove their pain. Jesus could be surprised, disappointed and hurt like any other man. Look up the following references and identify the nature of some of the trials that Jesus understands from firsthand experience.

A. Family Hurts - See Matthew 12:46-50 and John 7:1-5.

    _____
    _____
    _____

B. Home Church Hurts - See Matthew 13:54-58.

    _____
    _____
    _____

C. Ministry Team Hurts - See John 12:2-6; 13:2, 10-11, 21, 27.

    _____
    _____
    _____

D. Lack of Success Hurts - See John 1:11 with Luke 13:34-35 and 19:41-44

    _____
    _____
    _____

Persecutions in the Ministry - Part 1

Persecution can come in a broad variety of ways: accusations, conspiracy, confrontation, plots, mockery, physical injury, and so on. Jesus experienced all of them. Notice in the following passages how people sought to discredit and prevent him from fulfilling God's plans.

Matthew 9:32-34;
Luke 11:14-15; John 7:20;
8:48-52 and 10:19-20.

Matthew 21:23 and
John 8:12-18.

Matthew 12:38-42
and 16:1-4.

Persecutions in the Ministry - Part 2

Luke 7:31-35

Matthew 19:3-8; 22:15-22, 23-33, 34-40

Matthew 26:59-61

Matthew 27:26-30, 39-44

Why would any person persecute another person, especially the Son of God?
The answers may surprise you. You can locate them in these places:

Mark 15:9-10; John 12:1, 9-11

John 3:19-21

Putting It Together

Jesus knew that his mission among the Jews was largely doomed to fail and that he would be killed by them (Matt. 16:21-23; Mk. 10:32-34; Lk. 17:20-25). Nevertheless, "My food," said Jesus, "is to do the will of him who sent me and to finish his work" (Jn. 4:34). Based on the following Scriptures, how did Jesus get through the toughest ordeal of his life?

John 17:1-4 with Hebrews 12:2

_____
_____
_____
_____
_____

Hebrews 5:7-10 with Luke 22:39-46

_____
_____
_____
_____
_____
_____

Suffering of one kind or another comes to *every* spiritual leader. The sufferings that came against Jesus will also come against his followers . . . *against you*. Strangers, friends, family members and church members will love you one moment, then turn against you. You shouldn't be surprised by these disappointments. The sinful nature in people, coupled with the work of Satan, is certain to cross your path eventually (maybe more than several times!). The apostle Paul understood this agony more than once. In the end, it cost him his life. Read slowly the following inspiring words we have from Paul in his final correspondence:

The time has come for my departure.
I have fought the good fight,
I have finished the race,
I have kept the faith.
Now there is in store for me the crown of righteousness,
which the Lord, the Righteous Judge, will award to me on that day
— and not only to me, but also to all who have longed for his appearing!
2 Timothy 4:6-8

15952327R00030

Printed in Great Britain
by Amazon